Original title:
The Whispered Snow

Copyright © 2024 Swan Charm
All rights reserved.

Author: Liisi Lendorav
ISBN HARDBACK: 978-9916-79-897-3
ISBN PAPERBACK: 978-9916-79-898-0
ISBN EBOOK: 978-9916-79-899-7

Shivers of the Quiet Storm

The sky whispers low, paints shadows thin,
A hush lingers soft, where the night begins.
Stars flicker like dreams, lost in the mist,
Each heartbeat echoes, in twilight's twist.

Clouds dance in silence, a slow, gentle sway,
Carrying secrets, from the end of day.
Raindrops like whispers, fall calm on the ground,
In the quiet storm, solace is found.

Veils of Winter's Breath

Frost weaves its lace on the windowpane,
Breath of the cold, whispers sweet refrains.
Trees stand like sentinels, cloaked in white,
Guardians of dreams, in the still of night.

Footsteps muffled, on the soft, crisp snow,
Each step a story, in winter's glow.
In the chill of the air, there's warmth to find,
Veils of winter's breath, wrap the heart and mind.

Whispers Beneath the Drift

Beneath the soft drift, where silence resides,
Whispers awaken in twilight's tides.
Moonlight caresses the world so pale,
A dance of shadows, a tender tale.

Gentle winds carry, secrets through trees,
Rustling the branches, with soft, soothing pleas.
In the still is a magic, a world anew,
Whispers beneath the drift call out to you.

Secrets in the Frost

Crystals of frost lace the early dawn,
Hidden reflections where dreams are drawn.
Each breath a whisper, painted in air,
Secrets lie waiting, hidden with care.

The world shimmers bright, under starry skies,
With every soft glimmer, a truth gently lies.
In the stillness of morning, the stories unfold,
Secrets in the frost, a beauty untold.

Secrets of the Winter Veil

Whispers in the frosty air,
Stories lost with every flake,
Trees wear coats of glistening white,
Nature sleeps, but dreams awake.

Footprints lead to hidden paths,
A world wrapped in silver glow,
Silent echoes softly call,
In winter's hold, the secrets flow.

Branches bow with icy grace,
Each breath forms a fleeting cloud,
Underneath the blanket deep,
The earth dreams, silent yet proud.

Ethereal Silence in the Morning Light

Dawn creeps in with gentle touch,
Awakens all the frozen ground,
Shadows weave in golden threads,
A tranquil peace lies all around.

Glistening dew on every blade,
Nature's artwork, pure delight,
Whispers float on crisp, cool air,
As night retreats, yielding light.

Birds begin their morning song,
Harmonies of soft refrain,
In the hush, the world reborn,
Ethereal calm, free of pain.

Winter's Veiled Revelations

A shroud of white on every hill,
Secrets hidden in the snow,
Glimmers catch the morning sun,
Winter's magic starts to show.

Frosty breath and barren trees,
Nature speaks in silence deep,
Hidden worlds beneath the chill,
Winter whispers, hearts to keep.

The crystal dance of falling flakes,
Each one carries tales of old,
In their flight, the secrets stir,
In this silence, truths unfold.

The Secret Life of Flakes

Each flake forms a tale untold,
A dance that weaves through winter's chill,
Silent messengers of the storm,
In delicate patterns, they fulfill.

Softly landing on the ground,
Embracing every space they find,
Whirling through the biting air,
Letters written by the wind.

In their touch, a fleeting gift,
Moments caught before they melt,
A secret life within each flake,
A magic felt, but seldom dealt.

Melodies of a Chilled Silence

In the stillness, echoes play,
Whispers float on frozen air.
Crystals dance in soft ballet,
Nature's sigh, a solemn prayer.

Beneath the frost, dreams softly sleep,
Shadows linger, hushed and clear.
Quiet secrets, souls to keep,
In the night, the stars draw near.

Silent symphonies arise,
With each breath, the cold expanse.
Moonlight twinkles in the skies,
Calling forth the wild romance.

Breath of winter, crisp and bold,
Stories wrapped in silver light.
Ancient tales in silence told,
Every heartbeat feels so right.

In this world of frozen grace,
Every moment, pure delight.
Lost within this sacred space,
Melodies of the chilled night.

Winter's Hidden Whispers

Snowflakes drift on gentle breeze,
Softly landing on the ground.
Nature's voice, it comes with ease,
In this quiet, peace is found.

Subtle hints of springtime's glow,
Under layers, life will thrive.
In the stillness, hearts will know,
Winter's grace keeps dreams alive.

With each flake, a story spun,
Woven on the canvas white.
Every whisper, soft and fun,
Tells of warmth in cold's own light.

Footsteps echo, soft and slow,
Tracing paths of love and care.
In this chill, we come to know,
Winter speaks, and we must share.

All around, a world so bright,
Crafted by the frosty kiss.
Hidden truths in shadows light,
Hold the warmth of winter's bliss.

Glacial Echoes on a Moonlit Night

Underneath the silver dome,
Whispers glide on icy streams.
In the dark, the heart finds home,
As the night unfolds its dreams.

Glacial forms in gentle melt,
Chill the air, and calm the soul.
Every breath, a tale is felt,
Of the night, we are a whole.

Frozen lakes with secrets deep,
Hold the silence close and tight.
In this quiet, shadows creep,
As we dance in filtered light.

Moonbeams touch the snow-kissed ground,
Life awakens, bold and free.
In the hush, a sacred sound,
Nature's tune calls out to me.

Stars align in perfect rows,
Guiding dreams that drift and sway.
In this realm where magic grows,
Glacial echoes lead the way.

Snow's Gentle Tapestry of Secrets

Snowflakes weave a tale divine,
Covering the earth with care.
Threaded dreams in crystalline,
Showing beauty everywhere.

Each layer tells a silent tale,
Of the moments lost in time.
In their dance, the whispers sail,
Nature's rhythm, soft and prime.

Beneath the white, the world sleeps tight,
Cocooned in layers, warm and deep.
In the hush of the snowy night,
Secrets in the silence keep.

Glistening under starlit skies,
Every flake a work of art.
In their fall, a sweet surprise,
Brings the warmth to every heart.

Tapestries of frost and glow,
Wrap the earth in pure embrace.
In this quiet, slow we grow,
Snow's deep magic fills this space.

Soft Songs of the Chilling Breeze

Whispers sigh through the trees,
A gentle plea in the air,
Soft notes of winter's ease,
Embrace the world with care.

Clouds drift like memories,
Painting skies with gray hue,
The cold hums sweet melodies,
As secrets chase the blue.

Frosted grass holds the night,
Glistening under pale stars,
Every breath a soft light,
Guided by the moon's scars.

Through the lanes, shadows glide,
While silence holds its breath,
In a dance, none can hide,
Life entwined with death.

Hearts beat in muted chimes,
Wrapped in winter's soft hand,
Counting down the lost times,
In the quiet, we stand.

Echoes in the White Silence

Winter blankets the ground,
A soft quilt of pure snow,
In the stillness, a sound,
Whispers where cold winds blow.

Footsteps leave fleeting traces,
On paths both worn and new,
In this world, time embraces,
The silence deep and true.

A breath hangs in the air,
Carving frost on each breath,
Echoes of love and care,
A serene dance with death.

Snowflakes tap on the eaves,
Like secrets they cascade,
In the hush, our heart believes,
Such beauty won't soon fade.

Awake to morning's light,
The world glimmers with grace,
In the calm, pure delight,
Each moment finds its place.

Serenity on Frost-Laden Streets

Silent streets bathed in white,
Glow softly under the moon,
Each corner holds the night,
As dreams begin to croon.

Frost clings to every pane,
Crystals sparkling like stars,
Every breath a sweet refrain,
Painted echoes from afar.

Warmth bursts under thick coats,
As laughter fills the chill,
Hope sails on winter's boats,
Winding down each quiet hill.

While shadows stretch and play,
The heart finds peace in cold,
Golden hues start to sway,
As sunlight breaks the mold.

Serenity in each step,
A dance on icy ground,
In our hearts, secrets kept,
Where the stillness is found.

A Dance of Frosted Murmurs

Murmurs soft as morning mist,
Drift across the frozen lake,
Whispers of a fleeting tryst,
In silence, promises wake.

Frosted leaves gently sway,
Embracing the breath of air,
Nature's soft, unbroken play,
Flutters through the still affair.

Moonlight glints on the night,
Casting shadows, soft and true,
Each flicker, a promise bright,
Guiding dreams that weave through.

In the heart's quiet thrum,
Echoes of laughter ring wide,
Where frost and whispers hum,
A waltz that none can hide.

Time dances in the glow,
With every measured beat,
In the stillness, we flow,
Finding warmth in the sweet.

Secrets Carried by the Wind

Whispers float through the trees,
Carried softly on gentle breeze.
Promises made, lost in the air,
Secrets linger, no longer rare.

Chasing shadows in twilight's glow,
Hidden truths the wildflowers know.
Each rustle, a tale from the past,
In the silence, shadows are cast.

Voices echo where no one stands,
Stories written in shifting sands.
Nature keeps what we dare to hide,
As the wind becomes our confide.

Through valleys deep and mountains high,
The wind sings softly, a lullaby.
Worn-out memories intertwine,
A chorus of hearts, yours and mine.

With each gust, we learn to find,
The weight of words, the ties that bind.
In every whisper, a fragment stays,
Secrets carried in gentle ways.

White Memories on the Wind

Snowflakes tumble, softly they land,
Whitening hills, a silken strand.
Each flurry holds a blissful thought,
In the chill, sweet dreams are caught.

Childhood laughter fills the air,
Frosty moments, hearts laid bare.
Footprints trace through drifts of white,
With every step, a glance of light.

Cold air dances with warmth inside,
In this wonder, we can abide.
Ghosts of winter, bright and bold,
Stories wrapped in a blanket of cold.

As the twilight paints the sky,
Silver whispers seem to sigh.
Memories weave, both near and far,
Guided gently by the evening star.

These moments, fleeting, softly blend,
With every breeze, the tales extend.
In white memories, love takes flight,
Carried onward by wintry night.

A Quiet Dance of Ice

Crystal forms in shapes divine,
Quiet elegance, each edge aligns.
Underneath the moon's embrace,
A ballet forms, a timeless grace.

Frozen whispers fill the night,
Dancing softly, silver and white.
Each twinkle shines with stories old,
A silent dance, a sight to behold.

Twirling gently, down they fall,
Nature's grace, enchanting all.
In this stillness, worlds collide,
As the icy whispers glide.

Waltzing shadows, soft and sleek,
In the dark, the heart can speak.
Music flows through the frozen air,
A symphony of chill and flair.

Encased in beauty, life remains,
Where icy dreams transcend the plains.
In a quiet dance, silence grows,
As the magic of the winter glows.

Bated Breath of Winter Nights

Stars hang low, a velvet sky,
Frosted dreams in twilight lie.
Every breath a misty haze,
In the hush of winter's maze.

Softly falling, night descends,
Silent whispers, the darkness lends.
In the stillness, echoes play,
As the shadows melt away.

Warmth within this frozen realm,
Nature sways, we take the helm.
With each heartbeat, the world waits,
Bated breath, as fate creates.

The chill cradles stories old,
Silent tales, a heart unfolds.
Wrapped in warmth, beneath the stars,
Hopes and wishes, near and far.

In winter's grasp, we feel alive,
Holding close what we derive.
With bated breath, we cherish tight,
The magic woven through the night.

Serene Silence of the Winter's Embrace

In the hush where shadows play,
Snowflakes drift in soft ballet.
Trees stand tall, their branches bare,
A quiet peace fills the cold air.

Footsteps whisper on the ground,
Echoing the beauty found.
Winter wraps the world in white,
A tranquil pause in fading light.

The stillness holds a gentle grace,
Nature's mirror, a pale embrace.
Stars appear in evening's glow,
While the moon casts silver snow.

As frost adorns each window pane,
Life seems distant, free from pain.
In this calm, our hearts align,
Serenity, pure and divine.

Softly, dreams begin to rise,
Like the smoke in evening skies.
In winter's hold, the soul does sigh,
In serene silence, we comply.

Glistening Secrets of the Frigid Air

Glistening secrets in the night,
Whispers carried in twilight.
Breath of frost upon the breeze,
Mountain peaks and old, tall trees.

A symphony of soft refrains,
Echoing through the frosted plains.
Stars twinkle in a velvet sky,
While shadows dance and spirits fly.

Each crystal flake, a story spun,
Of winter's charm, when day is done.
Mirrored lakes reflect the past,
Nature's canvas, deep and vast.

With every gust, the secrets play,
In a world where time drifts away.
Music of the cold, so clear,
Calls to hearts, drawing them near.

In hidden paths where snowflakes fall,
We listen to winter's call.
Embrace the chill, the night's delight,
In glistening secrets, pure and bright.

A Veil of Frost and Whisper

A veil of frost drapes the dawn,
Whispers carried on the fawn.
Nature cloaked in icy lace,
Time stands still in this embrace.

Footsteps crunch on powdered ground,
The silence of the woods profound.
Each tree a statue, proud and grand,
Hiding secrets in this land.

Stars descend to touch the earth,
In winter's glow, there's endless worth.
With every breath, the chill ignites,
Painting dreams of endless nights.

Winds weave tales of days gone by,
Frosty kisses, a gentle sigh.
In each moment, a gift bestowed,
A veil of frost as hearts explode.

The world spins in a frosted dream,
A whisper soft, a silver seam.
In this magic, we find reprieve,
In winter's arms, we dare believe.

Heartfelt Whispers Among the Snowdrifts

Heartfelt whispers in the snow,
Where gentle winds of winter blow.
Among the drifts, a tale unfolds,
In every flake, a memory holds.

Paths entwined in white so deep,
Promises the winter keeps.
Laughter lingers in the air,
Every moment, fresh and rare.

Beneath the moon's soft, silvery light,
Love ignites on this starlit night.
Every word, a sacred trust,
Carried forward, as dreams must.

The air is filled with secret dreams,
In frozen streams, the world redeems.
With every heartbeat, hopes arise,
In winter's calm, we find the prize.

As dawn approaches, soft and clear,
Whispers linger, sweet and near.
In snowdrifts deep, we lose and find,
The heartfelt echoes left behind.

Frosty Breath of the Whispered Night

In the stillness, silence breathes,
Stars twinkle like frozen leaves.
Moonlight drapes a silver shawl,
Whispers echo, a gentle call.

Shadows dance on the ground,
In this beauty, peace is found.
Frosty edges kiss the trees,
Nature sways in the evening breeze.

Underneath the blanket white,
Dreams are born in the quiet night.
Time slows down, the world asleep,
While secrets in the cosmos seep.

Every breath a cloud released,
In this moment, worries ceased.
Voices soft, a tender prayer,
Frosty breath in the evening air.

A tranquil scene, the heart's delight,
Wrapped in warmth of frosted light.
In the night, a serene show,
Whispers fade, and all is snow.

Tides of Snow in the Whispering Wind

Snowflakes swirl on the chilling breeze,
Nature's dance among the trees.
Whispers travel on the air,
Softened moments, light as prayer.

Each flake tells a tale untold,
Of winters past, a thousand fold.
They drift like dreams on whispered sighs,
Filling hearts as the cold night flies.

The ground is dressed in the softest white,
A canvas bright beneath the night.
Tides of snow, both deep and light,
Painting silence with pure delight.

In every gust, secrets swirl,
As shadows dance and snowflakes twirl.
The hush of night brings gentle cheer,
In winter's arms, the world draws near.

With every breath, the chill ignites,
Echoing softly in frosty heights.
Tides of snow in dreamy blend,
Where every moment feels like a friend.

The Snow's Gentle Art of Silence

In winter's grasp, the world is hushed,
Soft snow falls, the landscape brushed.
A delicate layer, pure and bright,
The snow's gentle art, a soft light.

Each flake unique, a fleeting grace,
Covering all in a snow-white lace.
The silence sings a calming song,
In this embrace, we all belong.

Branches bow with their heavy load,
A tranquil path where footsteps strode.
In the depths of night, peace is found,
As stars glimmer, the snowflakes surround.

The world at pause, time seems to freeze,
In winter's canvas, calmness leaves.
The art of snow, a tender sigh,
Wraps the earth as moments fly.

So breathe in deep, let worries fade,
In nature's beauty, be unafraid.
The snow's soft whisper, a gentle balm,
In its embrace, the heart grows calm.

Chilling Whispers at Dusk

As shadows blend with night,
The wind begins to sigh,
Soft whispers from the trees,
A calm that draws us nigh.

Moonlight dances on the stream,
Casting dreams both bright and pale,
The world holds its breath, it seems,
In echoes of a tale.

Stars emerge like distant fire,
Each one a whispered wish,
Beneath the blanket deep,
Night's secrets softly swish.

A chill wraps round our hearts,
As night embraces dreams,
In the silence deep we part,
In whispers, nothing seems.

As dusk fades into night,
The twilight spirits dwell,
In chilling whisper of starlight,
Their message, soft and swell.

Hushed Tales of Winter's Silence

Snowflakes fall in gentle flight,
Blanketing the ground,
Each one a quiet story,
In silence, peace is found.

Trees stand tall, adorned in white,
Guardians of the night,
With branches stretched like arms,
A soothing, pure delight.

Fires crackle in the hearth,
While shadows dance around,
Each tale a whispered breath,
In winter's hush profound.

Footsteps fade in crisp, cold air,
Echoes lost to time,
In frosty breath we linger,
Nature's quiet rhyme.

With every gust of wind,
A tale woven so fine,
In winter's hush, we find,
The warmth that makes us shine.

Frosted Lullabies on the Ground

Underneath a frosty sky,
The world sleeps soft and low,
Blankets of white lullabies,
Whispering gentle flow.

Each blade of grass encased in ice,
A crystalline embrace,
The silent night serenades,
In nature's calm grace.

Dreams drift on the chilly breeze,
Carried far and wide,
Frosted dreams float softly down,
On winter's gentle tide.

Stars twinkle like lullabies,
Dancing in the sky,
Each note a whisper sweet,
As time slips quietly by.

In every tranquil moment,
A story made anew,
Frosted lullabies surround us,
In silence, pure and true.

Secrets Trapped in Icicles

Hanging crystal daggers shine,
Caught in winter's hold,
Each one keeps a secret safe,
In beauty, stark and bold.

Drips of water, hesitant,
A promise from the past,
Icicles cling, silent guards,
Their secrets locked so fast.

In sunlight, they sparkle bright,
Like diamonds in the air,
Yet beneath their glistening glow,
Lies a tale of despair.

As they melt, a drop escapes,
Carrying whispers clear,
Unraveling each hidden truth,
In silence we draw near.

Secrets whispered through the cold,
In each fragile frame,
Icicles hold the stories told,
Yet keep the heart the same.

Winter's Gentle Murmur

Snowflakes dance on the breeze,
Whispering secrets to the trees.
The world is wrapped in a soft embrace,
Silence lingers, a tranquil space.

Footprints mark the powdered ground,
A tapestry of peace is found.
Each breath releases a frosty sigh,
Under the vast and timeless sky.

Chill winds sing of seasons past,
In winter's art, memories cast.
The hearth glows bright, a warm retreat,
As night descends with quiet feet.

Stars peek through the shrouded night,
Twinkling softly, a wondrous sight.
In this realm of serene delight,
Winter whispers, pure and white.

Silence Beneath the Flurries

Gentle flakes drift down from above,
Each one a token of winter's love.
They blanket the earth in soft attire,
As trees stand guard, silent and dire.

The world grows still in beauty's breath,
As nature prepares for a peaceful death.
Whispers of frost caress the air,
In the midst of this wintry snare.

Footsteps echo in the snowy hush,
Through the woods, there comes a rush.
Wild creatures settle in their nests,
Seeking comfort in winter's quests.

A frozen lake mirrors the skies,
Reflecting dreams as daylight dies.
Under the weight of winter's night,
Silence reigns, a soft respite.

Luminescent Whispers of Winter

Moonlight kisses the fields so white,
A luminescent dance, pure delight.
Stars twinkle in the velvet dark,
Each one a whisper, a glowing spark.

Icicles hang from rooftops tall,
Catching glimmers as night starts to fall.
Frosted branches adorn the trees,
Swaying gently in the chilled breeze.

The hush of winter blankets the ground,
In the stillness, peace is found.
Below the surface, dreams do stir,
As the world waits for spring's warm blur.

Candles flicker in windows wide,
Offering warmth against the tide.
In the heart of winter's song,
Whispers of hope, where dreams belong.

The Language of Frost

Frost etches tales on window panes,
Stories told in crystalline chains.
Each pattern unique, a fleeting art,
A silent language that warms the heart.

Beneath a sky of muted gray,
The world transforms in a shimmering display.
Nature speaks in hushed tones,
A symphony played on winter's bones.

With every breath, the cold lingers near,
Carrying whispers for those who hear.
In the stillness, the earth will sigh,
As secrets of frost dance and fly.

Time holds its breath in this chilly air,
Moments are captured without a care.
The language of frost weaves its way,
Through the echoes of winter's sway.

The Sound of Ice Meeting Whisper

In the hush of frozen air,
A crackling tune unfolds,
Ice and silence weave a spell,
Nature's secrets softly told.

Whispers dance upon the pond,
Echoes glide on chilly beams,
Each ripple sings a fleeting song,
Crystalline dreams and frozen dreams.

Glistening shards reflect the light,
Stars trapped in frosted veins,
A symphony of cold and night,
In whispered tones, it remains.

The world holds its breath in awe,
Against the still, pure white,
The sound of ice meeting whisper,
A moment frozen in flight.

Beneath the Winter's Caress

Beneath the white and heavy shroud,
Life curls tight against the cold,
Each breath a cloud, a gentle vow,
In winter's arms, stories told.

The trees stand tall in silence deep,
Branches cradled by soft snow,
Dreams held close, as shadows creep,
Underneath the starry glow.

Frosted tips of blades of grass,
Glisten with the morning's kiss,
In this wonder, time will pass,
Yet in the chill, it feels like bliss.

A tapestry of azure skies,
Blanketed in whispers pale,
Beneath the winter's softest sighs,
We find warmth in the tale.

Frosted Whispers in Stillness

Frosted whispers glide through nights,
Bathed in silver, soft and clear,
Every spark a flickering light,
Caught in time, so precious here.

Stillness wraps the world in dreams,
Icicles hang with diamond grace,
Gentle echoes, like silent streams,
Tracing paths in night's embrace.

Frozen echoes, stories blend,
In the quiet, shadows twine,
Nature whispers, soft to lend,
Magic woven, pure, divine.

Footprints mark the snowy white,
As spirits dance with every breath,
Frosted whispers hold the night,
A serenade of life and death.

Secrets Wrapped in Winter's Breath

Secrets wrapped in winter's breath,
Carried on the icy stream,
Nature's hush, a whispered consort,
Weaving through the frosty dream.

Snowflakes fall like gentle sighs,
Layers deep, the world asleep,
Each one tells a tale of skies,
In frozen silence, secrets keep.

The moonlight casts a silver hue,
Upon the fields of glassy white,
Echoing the heart's soft view,
In winter's embrace, dreams ignite.

Beneath the stars, stillness reigns,
Boundless beauty, soft and grand,
In every flake, a world remains,
Winter's breath, a gentle hand.

Shadows of the Whispering Breeze

In the twilight's gentle grace,
Shadows dance in whispered trace.
Night's soft breath upon our skin,
Carrying secrets deep within.

Moonlight weaves through branches bare,
Filling hearts with lingering care.
A symphony of rustling leaves,
In the calm, the spirit weaves.

Echoes linger in the air,
Nature's heartbeat, pure and rare.
Each note a tale, each sigh a song,
A melody where we belong.

Stars above, they shimmer bright,
Guiding souls through velvet night.
In the shadows, dreams take flight,
Cradled in the arms of light.

As dawn breaks, shadows fade,
Yet the magic will not jade.
For in whispers, we will find,
The wind, our friend, forever kind.

Secrets of the Icy Aurora

Beneath the northern sky's embrace,
Colors dance with icy grace.
Glowing ribbons softly sway,
Whispering secrets of the day.

In the stillness, tales unfold,
Stories of the brave and bold.
Each flicker a memory cast,
In the heavens, shadows last.

Crimson, green, and depths of blue,
Painting night in shades anew.
A canvas spun from dreams and light,
Beneath the cosmic, endless night.

Quiet voices ride the winds,
Inviting hearts to make amends.
In the chill, the warmth will grow,
Ancient truths, the stars bestow.

So let us stand, embrace the glow,
As the icy winds of night blow.
In each beam, a whisper heard,
The aurora's heart, forever stirred.

The Quiet Gift of Winter's Touch

Frost-kissed fields in dawn's first light,
Silent beauty, pure and bright.
Each flake falls with softest grace,
Wrapping Earth in a gentle embrace.

Bare branches glisten, diamonds rare,
Nature's art beyond compare.
In the hush, a moment's peace,
Winter's breath brings sweet release.

Footsteps crunch on snowy ground,
In this realm, joy can be found.
Whispers of the wind convey,
Time's sweet pause on a winter's day.

Cozy warmth in hearth's soft glow,
Binding hearts in love's sweet flow.
Stories shared as fires crackle,
In winter's chill, our spirits wrackle.

When the world lies still and white,
Dreams awaken in the night.
The quiet gift of winter's touch,
Reminds us all to cherish much.

Silent Flakes Descend

Silent flakes descend so slow,
Covering the earth below.
Whispers soft, a magic spell,
In winter's grasp, we quietly dwell.

Each flake a flutter, soft and pure,
A fleeting moment to endure.
Nature's art, a choreographed dance,
Inviting all to take a chance.

Underneath a canopy white,
Lost becomes the heart of night.
In the quiet, dreams explore,
As silence lingers evermore.

Footprints mark a wandering trail,
While the cold winds softly wail.
In the stillness, peace is found,
As dreams take flight on frosted ground.

So let us pause, take a breath,
In the heart of winter's depth.
For in each flake that falls so free,
Lies the beauty of eternity.

Beneath the Glistening Blanket

Whispers of winter gently fall,
A soft embrace, a silent thrall.
Underneath the stars they lie,
A world transformed, a frozen sigh.

Footprints lost in drifts of white,
Shimmering strands in soft moonlight.
Each flake a story, brief yet bright,
Beneath the glistening, calm delight.

Trees adorned in icy lace,
Their branches bow, a graceful trace.
Echoing laughter, sweet and light,
Under the gaze of the quiet night.

Nature rests in whispered dreams,
Wrapped tightly in silvery schemes.
As shadows dance, they intertwine,
In this serene, celestial shrine.

Morning breaks, the mystery glows,
A vibrant world, as daylight shows.
The glistening blanket slowly fades,
Yet in our hearts, its beauty stays.

Murmurs in the Subtle Drift

The breeze carries secrets, soft and shy,
Rustling through leaves with a gentle sigh.
A dance of shadows upon the ground,
In every corner, a soft sound found.

Clouds drift lazily, a painter's stroke,
Weaving tales in wisps of smoke.
Each moment lingers, like a sweet kiss,
In this twilight world, we find our bliss.

Footsteps echo on the winding trail,
Dancing leaves, a fluttering veil.
Nature hums in quiet tunes,
Underneath the gaze of watchful moons.

Stars flicker like whispers in the dark,
Illuminating dreams with a fragile spark.
In the stillness, our hearts align,
Murmurs of magic, tender, divine.

As shadows lengthen, we drift and sway,
Lost in the moment, come what may.
In the subtle drift, we find our way,
Guided by sounds that softly play.

Lurking in the White Silence

In the depths of winter's breath,
A hush descends, a silencing sheath.
The world, a canvas, pure and still,
Whispers secrets against its will.

Crystals form in delicate art,
Intricate beauty, a frozen heart.
The shadows linger, soft and low,
In white silence, the mysteries flow.

Frost-kissed branches, a ghostly sight,
Nighttime cloaks with its shrouded light.
Echoes blend in the frosty air,
Lurking, waiting with timeless care.

Veils of mist draw near to play,
Softly drifting, they slip away.
In moments caught between the trees,
A world suspended in quiet ease.

As dawn approaches, colors wake,
This tranquil realm begins to break.
Yet in the heart, the stillness stays,
Lurking softly in winter's gaze.

Crystal Echoes at Dusk

As twilight drapes the sky in grace,
Clouds glow red in a gentle embrace.
The day whispers its soft goodbye,
Stars awaken in the dusky sky.

Reflections shimmer on the lake,
Each ripple tells of dreams we make.
In this moment, time stands still,
Crystal echoes, a beautiful thrill.

Among the pines, the shadows play,
Dancing lightly at the end of day.
Nature hums a calming tune,
Bathed in silver by the crescent moon.

Night unfolds like a delicate sheet,
Crickets chirp in a heartbeat.
The world adorned in twilight's kiss,
In crystal echoes, we find our bliss.

As starlight twinkles in depthless dreams,
We linger here, lost in moonbeams.
Each moment gleams with the softest trust,
Under the stars, the night's precious dust.

Whirling Whispers of Chill

In the breath of winter's night,
Whispers dance, a frosty flight.
Stars above twinkle and glow,
Casting dreams on earth below.

Branches sway in silent sighs,
Frosty patterns, soft and shy.
Nature wraps in purest white,
A world transformed, a wondrous sight.

Crystals glimmer, icy lace,
On the ground, a soft embrace.
Footsteps crunch, a symphony,
In the chill, a harmony.

Voices carried on the breeze,
Secrets tangled in the trees.
Drawn beneath the moon's soft glow,
Winter's song begins to flow.

Through the calm, the echoes flee,
Whirling whispers, wild and free.
In this hush, we find our way,
In the magic of the day.

Shadows of the Silver Veil

Moonlight filters through the trees,
Shadows dance on cool night's breeze.
Silver veil on winter's breath,
Whispers soft, a hint of death.

Branches creak in the still air,
Hidden secrets linger there.
Footsteps lost in softest snow,
Ancient tales the night winds blow.

Veiled in silence, dreams take flight,
Cloaked in shadows, soft and bright.
Wisps of fog entwine the ground,
In the hush, the lost are found.

Every flicker, every glance,
Echoes of a timeless dance.
In the night, they weave and wail,
A tapestry, the silver veil.

Glimmers fade at break of dawn,
But the whispers linger on.
In the light, the shadows fade,
Memories that twilight made.

Unveiling the Frozen Silence

In the stillness of the night,
Frozen silence, pure delight.
Wind's soft touch upon the skin,
Nature's breath, where dreams begin.

Blankets white on earth below,
Embracing all in gentle glow.
Every flake, a story told,
Of winter's magic, calm and bold.

Echoes linger, fade away,
Unraveling at break of day.
Boundless peace in every space,
Time sits still, a soft embrace.

Voices hush, the world holds breath,
A tranquil space between life and death.
As dawn awakens, colors play,
Unveiling dreams that melt away.

Frozen silence, deep and wide,
In the heart, the truth must hide.
Yet in stillness, we find grace,
In winter's calm, a sacred place.

Lullabies of the Falling Flakes

Snowflakes drift like whispered dreams,
In a world where silence gleams.
Each one dances, soft and light,
Lullabies that sing of night.

Gentle falls from skies above,
Cloaking Earth in peace and love.
Twirling, swirling, in midair,
A delicate, enchanting flair.

Children laugh, their voices bright,
Building snowmen, pure delight.
Joyful hearts in winter's play,
Nature's magic at display.

Timeless songs of peace resound,
In the hush, a warmth is found.
Falling flakes, a sweet refrain,
Carrying hopes like gentle rain.

As the world begins to sleep,
In the stillness, dreams we keep.
Nurtured by the moon's soft light,
Lullabies of purest night.

Crystalline Secrets of the Cold

In the hush of winter's breath,
Silent dreams of ice do weave.
Shimmers dance on frosted earth,
Whispers told to those who believe.

Glistening patterns in moonlight,
Each flake holds a story untold.
Nature's script of pure delight,
Crystalline secrets, brave and bold.

Frozen streams hold secrets deep,
Reflections caught in fragile glass.
Where time, like snow, can only leap,
Into the past, so softly, it will pass.

A world wrapped in a soft embrace,
Of winter's cloak, so pale and bright.
Each corner turned reveals a grace,
In this realm of pure delight.

The cold may bite, but hearts will warm,
Within this beauty, vast and grand.
Each crystalline shape takes form,
With magic spun by nature's hand.

Gentle Secrets Beneath the Snow

Beneath the blanket white and pure,
Lies a world of dreams concealed.
Silent whispers, soft and sure,
Gentle secrets yet revealed.

Snowflakes falling, soft caress,
Covering all with tender grace.
Winter's breath, a soft impress,
Hides the life in silent space.

Roots entwined in slumber's hold,
Awaiting spring's warm, sweet embrace.
Stories of the earth unfold,
In this tranquil, frozen place.

Above, the branches bow down low,
Cradling secrets in their arms.
Beneath the weight of falling snow,
Nature sleeps, away from charms.

As the sun begins to rise,
Melting dreams of white and gold.
A gentle sigh, the cold complies,
In the spring, new hopes unfold.

Frost-Kissed Echoes

In twilight's glow, the echoes play,
Frost-kissed whispers, soft and light.
Through the branches, shadows sway,
In the heart of winter's night.

Footsteps crunch on frozen ground,
Each sound a note in chilly air.
Nature's symphony is found,
In the stillness, everywhere.

Stars above like diamonds gleam,
Casting spells on silent skies.
In their light, the world may dream,
Hearing winter's lullabies.

Silent nights are full of grace,
Where the moonlight paints the way.
Every glimmer, every trace,
Frost-kissed echoes gently play.

Time stands still in winter's song,
Each moment wrapped in quiet bliss.
In this realm where hearts belong,
Frost-kissed echoes hold my wish.

Songs from the Frozen Whisper

From the depths of winter's song,
Whispers rise like clouds in flight.
Gently carried, soft and strong,
Songs of frost through silent night.

Every flake a note that falls,
Harmonies of cold embrace.
Nature sings, in snow-filled halls,
Melodies that time can't trace.

In the stillness, magic brews,
Voices rise on chilling breeze.
Stories told in frosty hues,
Echo softly through the trees.

As the dawn begins to break,
Colors burst in golden rays.
Songs of winter softly wake,
Promising the warmer days.

Yet for now, we cherish this,
Songs that dance on chilly air.
In the frost, a fleeting bliss,
Frozen whispers everywhere.

Softly Falling Hues of Winter

Softly falling shades of white,
Blanket trees in silent night.
Footprints whisper, stories told,
In the shimmer, dreams unfold.

Frozen lakes that mirror skies,
Glistening under starry sighs.
Gentle breezes softly sigh,
Watch the fleeting moments fly.

Icicles hang like silver thread,
Nature's artistry widespread.
In each flake, a tale resides,
Winter's beauty, calm abides.

Candles flicker, warmth inside,
As the twilight starts to glide.
Every shadow softly plays,
In the soft, embracing maze.

Whispers of the frosty air,
Linger sweetly everywhere.
Hearts entwined in winter's grace,
Find their peace in this embrace.

The Language of the Silent Ground

Underneath the blanket deep,
Nature's secrets softly seep.
Roots entwined in ancient lore,
Whisper tales forevermore.

Crickets hush as shadows blend,
In the dark, soft echoes mend.
Treading lightly on the seam,
Where the earth and magic dream.

Mossy stones hold history,
Telling tales of mystery.
Each step marks a silent vow,
To the past, we kneel and bow.

Patterns shift in the morning dew,
Nature's palette, ever new.
Through the veil of twilight's eyes,
Life emerges, softly tries.

Underneath the stars that gleam,
Silent stories start to stream.
In the night, the ground shall speak,
Yearning hearts, the truth they seek.

Songs of the Icy Woods

In the woods where silence reigns,
Nature hums its soft refrains.
Branches bow with crystal grace,
Echoes linger, time's embrace.

Snowflakes dance on gentle air,
Painting dreams without a care.
Watch the whispers of the trees,
Join the harmony with ease.

Footsteps crunched on snowy floors,
As the twilight softly pours.
Creatures pause, in shadows deep,
Guarding secrets that they keep.

Fragrant pine and icy breath,
Mark the balance 'twixt life and death.
In the stillness, all is clear,
Nature's music, we revere.

Listen close, the stories flow,
From the heart of winter's glow.
Each note carries pure delight,
In the songs of hushed twilight.

A Canvas of Frosted Whispers

A canvas painted, pale and bright,
Frosted whispers greet the night.
Every corner, wrapped in dreams,
Beneath the waning moonlight beams.

Veils of ice on windowpanes,
Catch the light, like silver chains.
Soft reflections, secrets glide,
In this chilly, gentle tide.

Nature's breath, a frosty art,
Carving beauty, every part.
In the silence, colors bloom,
Filling every empty room.

Wandering through this winter's grace,
Finding magic in the space.
Every whisper softly calls,
In the frost, enchantment sprawls.

With each step, new wonders rise,
Captured in the starlit skies.
A canvas vast, forever pure,
In the beauty, we find cure.

Murmurs on the Frosted Ground

Whispers weave through frozen grass,
Soft as dreams that come to pass.
Footfalls light on chilly air,
Nature sleeps without a care.

Moonlit glimmers on the snow,
Silent paths where shadows flow.
Each breath hangs like fragile lace,
Marking time in winter's space.

Crackling twigs beneath the weight,
Echoes softly, sealing fate.
Murmurs rise and softly fall,
Frosted ground, a sacred hall.

In the stillness, secrets bind,
Winter's heart to those aligned.
Every step, a tale to tell,
Murmurs weave a magic spell.

As the dawn begins to glow,
Melodies in sunlight flow.
Frosty murmurs fade away,
Bringing light to greet the day.

Secrets in the Winter Breeze

The winter breeze, a gentle sigh,
Carries secrets from the sky.
Each flake dances, tales in flight,
Whispers wrapped in soft, pure white.

Trees stand guard with icy crowns,
Silent sentinels in towns.
Branches bend to hear the song,
Voices minimal but strong.

Footprints etched in morning's chill,
Stories fade, but echoes will.
Breathe the air, crisp and divine,
Secrets linger like fine wine.

As stars twinkle, night unfolds,
The breeze shares treasures untold.
Every gust, a fleeting friend,
Whispering of where we bend.

With each breath, a hush so sweet,
In the winter, spirits meet.
Listen close, let silence tease,
Unravel secrets in the breeze.

Gentle Hush of Winter's Veil

Softly falls the winter's veil,
Blanketing the earth so pale.
Whispers hush in snow's embrace,
Time slows down, a sacred space.

Frosty breath on windowpanes,
Nature's art in crystal chains.
Every flake, a story spun,
Silent dances, one by one.

In the twilight, shadows blend,
Gentle hush, a timeless friend.
Life retreats to rest and dream,
In the stillness, we redeem.

Beneath the quiet, truths arise,
Winter's whispers, pure and wise.
Hold them close, let your heart feel,
The gentle hush of winter's veil.

As the world drifts into sleep,
Nature's promise softly keeps.
Underneath the frosty glow,
Secrets bloom in silent snow.

Echoes Beneath the Icy Canopy

Beneath the canopy of frost,
Echoes linger, never lost.
Softly glowing in the night,
Nature's chorus, pure delight.

Branches weave a crystal maze,
Catching light in winter's gaze.
Every breath a cloud of white,
Heartbeat echoes, pure and bright.

Frozen rivers, quiet flows,
Tales from depths the mind bestows.
Whispers travel through the trees,
Carried gently on the breeze.

In the stillness, peace enfolds,
Echoes dance as silence scolds.
Each moment wrapped in layered sound,
Life persists beneath the ground.

Underneath this magic dome,
Every heart can find a home.
Listen close to hear the call,
Echoes beneath the icy thrall.

Gentle Crystals of Silent Night

Gentle crystals softly gleam,
Beneath a sky of velvet dream.
Each sparkle tells a whispered tale,
Of winter's grace and icy veil.

The moonlight dances on the snow,
Creating paths where night winds blow.
In this silence, hearts take flight,
Wrapped in warmth of silent night.

Stars above in twinkling light,
Guide the dreams that take their flight.
Each breath a cloud, so pure and bright,
As we embrace the tranquil night.

Time stands still in snowy fields,
Where nature's beauty gently yields.
A world transformed, so calm and white,
In the hush of soft moonlight.

Let the night cradle your fears,
As the dawn approaches near.
In gentle crystals, peace takes flight,
In the heart of silent night.

Frosty Whispers at Dawn

Frosty whispers greet the morn,
As the sun begins to adorn.
A world awash in icy haze,
Shimmers bright in golden rays.

Nature stirs with quiet grace,
Birds awaken, find their place.
Each note a gentle, lilting sound,
In the magic all around.

The ground reflects a silver sheen,
As shadows stretch, and day is seen.
Each blade of grass, a work of art,
Warmth encroaches, steals the heart.

With every step, a crunch below,
Frosty whispers, softly flow.
Embrace the chill, the morning bright,
As dawn breaks forth with pure delight.

In the stillness, dreams unfurl,
As nature dances, swirls and swirls.
Frosty whispers at dawn's light,
Bring a promise, fresh and bright.

Shadows in the Midnight Frost

Shadows lurk in midnight frost,
Whispers of the day now lost.
Gleaming ice like diamonds rare,
Hides the secrets everywhere.

Footsteps muffled, silent night,
Every corner holds a fright.
Yet in shadows, beauty sighs,
Underneath the starlit skies.

Trees stand tall, their limbs adorned,
With icy lace, as if reborn.
In this dark, a chill breathes slow,
A dance of shadows, ebb and flow.

The moon peeks through the evening veil,
Casting down its silver trail.
In the frost, a story told,
Of midnight secrets, brave and bold.

As silence wraps the world in grace,
Moments linger, time and space.
Shadows in the frost invite,
A marvelous, enchanting night.

Beneath a Blanket of Stillness

Beneath a blanket, soft and light,
Stillness cradles the world so tight.
Each flake descends with gentle grace,
Covering earth in a cozy embrace.

A hush envelops all around,
As peace descends without a sound.
In the depth of this frozen calm,
Nature whispers, sweet and warm.

The stars above begin to fade,
As dawn approaches, unafraid.
In the stillness, life will bloom,
A promise held beneath the gloom.

Birds will chirp, and children play,
In the light of a brand new day.
But in this moment, stay awhile,
Wrapped in stillness, breathe and smile.

Beneath a blanket, close your eyes,
Feel the warmth as silence flies.
In stillness, let your heart take flight,
Beneath the calm of soft twilight.

Veils of Frozen Serenity

Veils of white whisper low,
Blanketing the world below.
In silence deep, the shadows play,
As night drapes its gentle sway.

Stars flicker in the endless sky,
Each one a wish that drifts on high.
The breath of frost curls in the air,
A tranquil peace, a moment rare.

Nature pauses, time stands still,
In this realm, the heart can fill.
With crisp echoes of the hue,
Of winter dreams, serene and true.

Branches clad in crystal lace,
Hold secrets of this frozen place.
Moonlight dances on the ground,
In this magic, peace is found.

Here lost worries gently fade,
In the stillness, fears cascade.
Veils of serene frost entwine,
In nature's cradle, all is fine.

Soft Shivers in the Glistening Quiet

Soft shivers brush against the skin,
As night wraps the earth in a win.
Glistening flakes fall without sound,
A peaceful world, beauty unbound.

In the quiet, whispers play,
Ghosts of winter dance and sway.
Each flurry tells a tale untold,
As dreams of warmth in hearts unfold.

Beneath the stars, the trees stand tall,
Encased in beauty, embracing all.
Chilling winds caress the night,
Every shadow holds a light.

In this stillness, time does cease,
Fleeting moments bring a peace.
With every breath, the magic grows,
In this cold, the spirit glows.

Soft shivers cradle the mind,
In the quiet, solace we find.
A winter's breath, gentle and near,
Wraps us close, calms every fear.

Chilling Whispers of the Past

Chilling whispers float on air,
Stories trapped in silence rare.
Echoes linger, hearts ensnare,
In the twilight, shadows stare.

Footsteps crunch on frosted ground,
In every sound, memories abound.
The past entwined with time and snow,
In these moments, spirits grow.

Frozen tales of love and loss,
Each breath a sigh, a gentle cross.
In whispers, ghostly voices blend,
As frigid winds anoint and mend.

The moon appears, a silver guide,
Unveiling secrets that abide.
Chilling thoughts of yesteryears,
In silence shared, dissolve our fears.

Chilling whispers softly call,
In the quiet, we recall.
A tapestry of life once cast,
Woven deep in winter's grasp.

Snowbound Secrets in Twilight

Snowbound secrets softly sigh,
Underneath the twilit sky.
Each flake a story yet to share,
In frozen time, they linger there.

Twilight's brush paints world anew,
In shades of blue, a tranquil hue.
Hidden paths of dreams take flight,
As day morphs into the night.

Sparkling tendrils weave and twist,
Glimmers touch what once was missed.
Veils of frost and shadows blend,
Whispers of the night transcend.

In this hush, we pause and breathe,
Finding warmth in tales we weave.
Snowbound secrets held so tight,
Whispered softly into the night.

As stars awaken one by one,
Revealing what the day has spun.
Snowbound dreams in twilight's glow,
In stillness, all the wonders flow.

Silent Flurries

Snowflakes whisper, softly fall,
Blanketing the earth in quiet thrall.
The world is hushed, a lullaby,
As gentle flurries dance and sigh.

Beneath the trees, a blanket white,
Each crystal sparkles in the night.
Footprints vanish, lost in time,
In this moment, pure and prime.

Winds weave tales, secrets spun,
Of winter's charm, of day undone.
Each breath of frost, a fleeting kiss,
In silent flurries, find your bliss.

The moon ascends, a silver gleam,
Illuminating dreams that teem.
Nature slumbers, calm and still,
In snowy realms, the heart can fill.

So linger here, let worries cease,
Embrace the hush, the quiet peace.
In silent flurries, joy unfurls,
A moment's magic, as time whirls.

Echoes in White

In the stillness, whispers rise,
Echoes linger 'neath the skies.
A canvas stretched in purest hue,
Winter's breath, a song anew.

Each flake a note, a tale retold,
Stories of warmth in the bitter cold.
Footsteps print the fragile ground,
In echoes soft, where dreams abound.

Branches bowed with heavy grace,
Nature dons a frosted lace.
In silence deep, there's music played,
An orchestra in white arrayed.

Time slows down, a gentle pause,
In winter's grasp, without a cause.
Hear the echoes, faint and bright,
A symphony in shades of white.

Let your heart find peace and light,
In the dreamscape of the night.
With every echo, let it be,
A moment shared in reverie.

Frost's Gentle Murmur

Frost paints softly on the glass,
Nature's art, a fleeting pass.
With every line, a story traced,
In morning light, its charms embraced.

Whispers swirl in chilly air,
As silence dances everywhere.
The world awakes in crystal clinks,
In frost's embrace, the spirit winks.

A soft murmur, the trees respond,
To winter's touch, to dreams beyond.
Each breath we take, a misty sigh,
In gentle murmurs, thoughts can fly.

Beneath the sky, so vast and wide,
Gentle moments, hearts coincide.
In every chill, a warmth will grow,
Frost's gentle murmur, a tender flow.

So let the frost enchant your soul,
Embrace the still, become whole.
In nature's hush, find endless grace,
In the murmur, a sweet embrace.

Dreams in the Drifting

Dreams take flight in drifting snow,
A tapestry where wishes flow.
In silent realms, they weave and twine,
In winter's grasp, all hearts align.

Beneath the stars, the world ignites,
A dance of dreams in winter nights.
Each flake a wish, each drift a prayer,
In the quiet, souls laid bare.

Time unfurls in snowy light,
As dreams unfold in soft twilight.
Embers glow in the frozen air,
A warmth within, beyond compare.

Let whispers guide you on your way,
Through enchanted nights and frosty day.
With every drift, another chance,
To find your peace in winter's dance.

So close your eyes, let visions soar,
In dreams that drift forevermore.
In the quiet, a promise held,
In snowy dreams, love is compelled.

The Soft Secret of Winter's Breath

Whispers weave through the icy air,
Soft secrets carried without a care.
Each flake dances on a breeze so light,
Embracing the world in hush of white.

Silent trees wear a coat of frost,
In their beauty, no warmth is lost.
Stars twinkle through a shroud so fine,
Kindling dreams in the night's design.

Frozen lakes hold reflections dim,
The moon glows gently, edges slim.
Footsteps muffled in the blanket deep,
Winter's breath beckons for us to keep.

A world transformed in peaceful peace,
Where time slows down, worries cease.
The soft secret of winter's embrace,
Unraveling warmth in this chilly space.

Snowflakes sing in soft refrain,
A lullaby where dreams remain.
Each moment still, the heart finds rest,
In winter's breath, forever blessed.

Murmurings in a Frozen Dreamscape

Soft murmurs echo through the night,
In this frozen dreamscape, pure and bright.
Stars glance down with a twinkling eye,
A canvas of wonder in the sky.

Pine trees whisper ancient tales,
As flurries swirl in gentle gales.
Each breath steams, a fleeting sign,
In the quiet night where spirits dine.

Nights drape shadows, cool and deep,
Secrets linger where shadows creep.
The moon ignites the snow-kissed ground,
In a silence, profound and sound.

Time pauses in this wintry trance,
Inviting all to join the dance.
A moment captured, pure delight,
In murmurings soft throughout the night.

Dreamers find solace in the chill,
As frost embraces with gentle thrill.
In this dreamscape where wonders sweep,
Murmurings beckon us into sleep.

Awe of the Silent Snowfall

In awe of the silent snowfall laid,
A blanket of white, both soft and stayed.
Each flake joins in a delicate ballet,
Transforming the earth in a gentle way.

The world pauses, wrapped in peace,
Movement slows, tensions cease.
Grey skies cradle this tranquil sight,
Holds the heart in pure delight.

Footprints wander through drifts divine,
In the magic, the stars align.
Each breath of cold, a crisp embrace,
In this silence, we find our place.

Branches sag under nature's weight,
Every limb dressed, no need to wait.
Time stands still as the beauty falls,
In the hush of winter's soft calls.

The heart reflects on moments pure,
In the awe of snowfall, we endure.
A tranquil world where all can see,
The silent wonders, wild and free.

Chilling Symphony of Soft Flakes

Hear the chilling symphony at play,
As soft flakes drift and sway.
In harmony, they paint the ground,
Creating silence, a soothing sound.

Winter's breath commands the chill,
Every flake fulfills its thrill.
A canvas wide where dreams converge,
In chorus, delicate flakes emerge.

Whirling gently in the frosty air,
Nature's magic boldly laid bare.
Each flake tells a tale anew,
In this symphony, both bright and blue.

Along the path of shadowed night,
Soft flakes twinkle in silver light.
Every moment, a masterpiece unfolds,
In the silence, a warmth that holds.

Listening closely to winter's tune,
In each soft flake, a gentle boon.
A chilling symphony, sweetly composed,
Winter's embrace forever exposed.

Surrendered to the Soft White Gaze

In the hush of falling snow,
The world wraps in a gentle glow.
Whispers dance on frosty air,
A silent promise, light as prayer.

Footprints fade on white abyss,
Every moment feels like bliss.
Nature's quilt, a soft embrace,
Inviting all to slow the pace.

Trees stand tall with branches bare,
Carrying secrets they cannot share.
The soft white gaze ignites the night,
Guiding hearts with purest light.

Children laugh, their joy in flight,
Snowflakes twirl, a pure delight.
Life unfolds in muted tones,
Surrendered to the softest zones.

Time stands still beneath the sky,
As dreams and wishes softly sigh.
In this trance, we find our way,
Surrendered to the soft white sway.

When the World Turns Soft

Whispers of dusk gently descend,
A world once harsh begins to bend.
Colors fade, but warmth remains,
In the soft, a peace sustains.

Clouds embrace the fading light,
Day slips softly into night.
All the edges lose their might,
When the world turns soft and bright.

Wildflowers sway in evening's grace,
No hurry now, just a gentle pace.
The rush of life, a distant call,
In softness, we can have it all.

Paths unwound in twilight's fold,
Stories shared and dreams retold.
Hearts attune to the silence sweet,
When the world turns soft, we meet.

Time dissolves in shadows long,
Wrapped in peace like a soothing song.
Each moment glows with tender might,
When the world turns soft, all feels right.

Shadows of Winter's Lullaby

In the depths of winter's night,
Moonlight casts a silver light.
Quiet whispers fill the air,
Shadows weave without a care.

Boughs adorned with icy lace,
Nature cradles time and space.
Frosty breath on windowpanes,
Winter sings in soft refrains.

Crickets hush, their song put down,
Snowflakes spin without a sound.
Each breath a crystal moment's tease,
Shadows dance with playful ease.

A lullaby for hearts so still,
Calm descends, a soothing thrill.
In the dark, there's light to find,
Shadows weave what dreams unwind.

Here beneath the starlit skies,
Winter's hush brings gentle sighs.
Wrapped in warmth, we find a way,
In shadows of winter's sway.

Winter's Hidden Conversations

Amidst the snowflakes' soft descent,
Nature whispers, secrets bent.
Snowdrifts speak in silent tones,
Winter's breath on ancient stones.

Bare branches lift their arms in prayer,
Talking to the frosty air.
Every freeze unveils a tale,
Caught in time like a ship's sail.

Creatures stir beneath the frost,
Life persisting, never lost.
In the stillness, stories gleam,
Winter's heart holds every dream.

A crackling fire, warmth and light,
Listen close to night's delight.
In hushed tones, when silence reigns,
Winter's hidden song remains.

Stars above join in the dance,
Symbolizing hope and chance.
In the cold, new worlds arise,
Winter's conversations, wise.

Frostbitten Secrets in the Night

Under the stars, the cold winds sigh,
Moonlight dances, shadows lie.
Silent whispers under frozen breath,
Frostbitten secrets of life's quiet death.

Snowflakes flutter, each unique flight,
Carving patterns in the dark of night.
Echoes of laughter lost in despair,
Smothered beneath the chill of the air.

Beneath the frost, stories untold,
Memories wrapped in blankets of cold.
Time stands still in this icy space,
Frostbitten secrets, a fleeting trace.

The stillness deepens, the world's asleep,
In this silence, the heart begins to weep.
Frozen dreams beneath layers of snow,
Frostbitten whispers, as time moves slow.

Yet in the twilight, warmth may still bloom,
Hope lingers softly amidst the gloom.
With every dawn, we chase away fright,
Unveiling the truths of the frostbitten night.

The Cacophony of Crystalline Whispers

Amidst the woods, a symphony plays,
Crystalline whispers in frosty array.
Each flake a note, a delicate sound,
Dancing on branches, where beauty is found.

In the hush of night, echoes ignite,
A cacophony blooms in shimmering light.
Nature's canvas, a magical sphere,
Whispers unfolding in crisp, crystal clear.

Frozen melodies spin through the air,
Harmonious murmurs, gentle and rare.
Every shimmering edge holds a tale,
As whispers weave softly, like snowflakes frail.

The moon casts shadows, a silver embrace,
Each crystalline note finds its rightful place.
In the depths of winter, we listen and see,
The beauty in chaos, as wild as can be.

Yet deep in the heart of this chilling refrain,
Lies warmth beneath, shelter from pain.
For every whisper that dances on ice,
A flicker of hope in the cold, so precise.

Still Reflection of White Wonders

In stillness wrapped, the world lies bright,
White wonders shimmer in the soft twilight.
Mirrored on lakes, the heavens descend,
Nature reflects, as day starts to end.

Gentle snowflakes drift, silent glide,
Painting the landscape, a heaven-wide.
Each moment captured in a crystal frame,
The purity of silence, nature's own name.

Trees adorned in lace, a quiet delight,
Glowing softly under pale moonlight.
Wanders of white envelop the ground,
In this tranquil hush, serenity found.

Reflections linger in the mind's eye,
As dreams weave softly through the night sky.
Frozen stillness, a beautiful trance,
White wonders whisper, inviting to dance.

As dawn approaches, gold hues will gleam,
But still in our hearts, we hold this dream.
For the beauty of white, in stillness enshrined,
Echoes forever in the soul of mankind.

Whispers of the Glacial Night

Under the veil of a glacial night,
Soft whispers travel, wrapping in white.
Every sigh of the earth draws near,
Echoes of mysteries, easy to hear.

Stars twinkle softly, their secrets unfold,
Sharing the stories the night has told.
In icy embrace, the world starts to dream,
Tranquil and quiet, like a gentle stream.

The frost-kissed air creates a soft tune,
Woven from shards of the bright silver moon.
Each breath held captive in the winter's hold,
Whispers of glacial wonders unfold.

Silhouettes dance where shadows reside,
With the chill of the night as a comforting guide.
As morning approaches, the whispers take flight,
Carried away by the breath of the night.

Yet in our hearts, these whispers remain,
The magic of winter, a soothing refrain.
Alive in our souls as we journey and roam,
Whispers of the glacial night call us home.

The Glistening of Untold Stories

In shadows deep, tales softly weave,
Whispers of dreams held tight, believe.
Every glance a spark, ignites the night,
Unraveled secrets catch the light.

Through ages past, voices intertwine,
Painting worlds where hearts align.
Ink that flows like a river's grace,
Bears the weight of a hidden place.

A tapestry of moments spun,
Infinite paths where hearts have run.
Each stitch a life, vibrant and bold,
Stories glisten, waiting to be told.

When silence speaks, a feeling grows,
The beauty in all that no one knows.
Time's gentle hand, a careful guide,
In every shadow, truths abide.

So gather round, lend an open ear,
For every story holds a tear.
Underneath the stars, we all belong,
To the glistening tales, life's sweet song.

Frost-Kissed Whimsies

Dancing flakes on winter's breath,
Frost-kissed whimsies beyond death.
Whispers of joy in the silent air,
Each flurry trembles with gentle care.

A twinkling world wrapped in white,
Morning glimmers, a soft delight.
Trees wear jewels that sparkle bright,
Crystals twirl in the soft twilight.

Paths of ice in sunlit dreams,
Echoes of laughter, joyful screams.
Children play in a frosted maze,
In this stillness, the heart shall gaze.

Every snowflake tells a tale,
Of crisp adventures, sweet and frail.
Magic lives in a world so pure,
Frost-kissed whimsies, hearts endure.

With every breath, the secrets flow,
In frozen realms, our spirits glow.
For in the chill, we find the warm,
A dance of life, in winter's charm.

Beneath the Shimmering White

Under blankets of silent snow,
Dreams lay hidden, lying low.
Nature whispers in hushed tones,
Beneath the white, life softly moans.

The world transforms, a canvas bright,
Each flake holding memories tight.
Frozen wonders, embracing night,
Guiding us to a soft insight.

Stars above, like diamonds shine,
Casting wishes in every line.
Beneath the shimmer, hopes awake,
In every heart, a path we stake.

Time drapes shadows, moments sway,
While nature's heartbeat fades away.
In the stillness, we seek to find,
Truths unwoven by fate, entwined.

So cherish the calm, embrace the cold,
For there are stories yet untold.
Beneath the shimmering white, we roam,
Finding warmth, together, at home.

Murmurs of the Frozen Earth

In the stillness, secrets linger,
Murmurs soft, they touch a finger.
Frozen earth breathes tales of yore,
Whispers echo, forevermore.

Crystals form in moonlit dreams,
Nature's heart in silent beams.
Underneath, the stories grow,
Echoes of life, and time's soft flow.

Footsteps on snow tell where we've been,
Paths of wanderers, lost in skin.
Each beat of frost, a heartbeat's mark,
A legacy sheltered in the dark.

Through layers deep, the voice of night,
Calls us forth to share our light.
In frozen whispers, we must stand,
For the earth holds tales, softly planned.

So listen close, let spirits soar,
For murmurs of life reach out for more.
In the echoes of the earth's refrain,
We find our place, again, again.

Shimmering Tales from Nature's Embrace

In the forest deep, where echoes dwell,
Whispers of leaves weave a vibrant spell.
Dancing shadows play on the ground,
Nature's heartbeat is a soothing sound.

Rivers glisten under the sun's warm gaze,
Painting reflections in a golden haze.
Mountains stand tall, a silent keep,
Guardians of secrets the wild things reap.

Flowers bloom bright in a riot of hues,
Breath of the earth in the morning dews.
Each petal tells of stories untold,
In nature's embrace, the magic unfolds.

Stars twinkle down from a velvet sky,
Each one a story that wishes to fly.
Nightingale sings a soft lullaby,
Under the moon, dreams drift and sigh.

Oceans whisper on the sandy shore,
Waves carve their tales forevermore.
In nature's arms, our souls find peace,
Shimmering tales that will never cease.

A Serenade of Snowflakes

Delicate dancers from the heavens above,
Whirling softly, a winter's love.
Each flake a promise, a wish in flight,
Transforming the world to a canvas of white.

Silence blankets the earth so deep,
In the hush of snow, the world seems to sleep.
Footprints echo, a soft, gentle trace,
In this enchanted, snowy embrace.

Branches adorned with glistening grace,
Nature's jewels in a frozen embrace.
A symphony quiet, a magical show,
As each snowflake dances down low.

Fires crackle, glowing bright,
Inside, we share warmth through the night.
Outside, the air is crisp and clear,
As we greet winter with laughter and cheer.

As dawn breaks, the sunlight cascades,
Turning snowflakes to shimmering cascades.
A serenade echoes, soft like a sigh,
In the heart of winter, we learn to fly.

Hushed Instants of Wintertime

In the stillness, time seems to pause,
Winter's breath, a moment that draws.
Frost-kissed mornings, so quiet and bright,
Dreams delicately woven in shimmering light.

Pine trees whisper secrets of snow,
Softly embracing the chill below.
Branches laden, bending low,
Nature's quiet beauty, an artful show.

Icicles hang like chandeliers grand,
Glistening treasures in a white wonderland.
Each instant a treasure, a fleeting sight,
Capturing moments in the soft twilight.

Crisp air fills lungs with a chilly delight,
As snowflakes tumble in the pale moonlight.
Each flake whispers tales of old,
In hushed instants, magic unfolds.

Through frosted windows, we gaze in awe,
At the beauty outside, nature's law.
In every hush, a heartbeat slows,
Wintertime whispers where tranquility flows.

Snowy Reveries in the Crystalline Still

Wrapped in white, the world feels surreal,
Each flake a dream that nature can steal.
Footsteps muted, a soft, gentle thrill,
Crisp air abounds in the crystalline still.

The landscape glows with a pearly sheen,
Every corner a sight, like a timeless scene.
Silvery whispers beckon and call,
In snowy reveries, we lose and enthrall.

Children's laughter, joy all around,
Creating memories in the snow-covered ground.
Snowmen stand proud with carrots for noses,
Each giggle a melody as winter encloses.

The sky blushes pink as day turns to night,
Stars peek through blankets, a twinkling sight.
The world slows down, a magical glow,
In this perfect moment, love starts to grow.

In the hush of winter, dreams intertwine,
Each snowy reverie, a rich design.
Captured in time, our hearts gently thrill,
In the serene embrace of the crystalline still.

Cold Breath of the Whispering Wind

The icy breath does softly creep,
Through barren trees where shadows leap.
It whispers tales of winter's chill,
And sends cold shivers through the hill.

A dance of frost in twilight's glow,
Each gust reveals what none could know.
It stirs the heart, it calls the night,
A haunting song of pure delight.

Around the corners, memories swirl,
Of frozen dreams in winter's whirl.
The wind reclaims what time forgot,
In its embrace, all warmth is caught.

With every breeze, a story shared,
Of quiet moments, hearts bared.
In whispered tones, the secrets flow,
The cold breath's kiss, a gentle glow.

So listen close when silence reigns,
For in the wind, true beauty gains.
From icy plains to starry skies,
The whispering wind never lies.

Luminous Silence of the Falling Snow

In midnight still, the snow descends,
A blanket soft that gently bends.
Each flake a pearl from heavens high,
Whispers of calm that drift and sigh.

The world transforms, a hush profound,
In luminous silence, beauty's found.
Each step a careful dance with grace,
The quiet drapes in nature's embrace.

Moonlit paths where shadows gleam,
The snowflakes swirl, a fleeting dream.
Their gentle fall, a symphony,
Composes peace for you and me.

Time seems to pause, a sacred prayer,
In stillness wrapped, we breathe the air.
Luminous silence kisses the night,
While snowflakes shimmer in soft light.

With every drift, a story spun,
Of winter nights and days undone.
In this embrace, we find our way,
In sparkling whispers, night and day.

An Ode to the Frozen Silence

Upon the ground, a blanket sprawls,
In frozen hush, the evening calls.
Each crystal shines with purest light,
An ode to silence wrapped in white.

The trees stand tall, their branches bare,
In stillness found, a world laid bare.
Whispers of frost greet every sigh,
As secrets linger in the sky.

A tapestry of icy dreams,
Where nature sings in silver streams.
In frozen peace, our spirits blend,
An ode to silence, time suspend.

With every breath, the cold we take,
Awakens wonder, hearts awake.
In frozen realms, we find our song,
An ode to stillness, deep and long.

So let us wander, hand in hand,
Through frosty fields where dreams are planned.
In frozen silence, love will find,
A bond unbroken, heart entwined.

Soft Shroud of Winter's Murmurs

Beneath a shroud of winter's grace,
A tapestry woven, time's embrace.
Each whisper soft, a tale to weave,
In murmurings of dreams we believe.

The snowflakes dance on winter's breath,
A gentle hush that speaks of depth.
With every flake, the world anew,
In softest whispers, life shines through.

The forest sleeps, a still retreat,
Wrapped in silence, the world's heartbeat.
From branches bare, to fields of white,
The murmurings echo through the night.

In winter's arms, we find reprieve,
In softest sounds, we dare to believe.
A shroud of peace, a gentle touch,
In winter's whispers, we feel so much.

So listen close, the echoes call,
A symphony wrapped, winter's thrall.
In soft shrouds of murmurs, we find
The essence of love, unconfined.

Softness of the Cold Embrace

Whispers descend on frosty eve,
A blanket of snow, the heart believes.
Gentle shadows dance in the chill,
Silent secrets, the night does fill.

Stars twinkle in the velvet sky,
Embracing the earth as time drifts by.
In this stillness, warmth finds a way,
In the cold's grasp, we softly stay.

Breath misting in the frozen air,
Each heartbeat echoes, a silent prayer.
With nature's touch, we come alive,
In the cold embrace, together we thrive.

Moonlight kisses the winter ground,
In her glow, lost souls are found.
Each flake that falls is a tender sigh,
In the softness, love can never die.

So let us linger in this serene space,
Wrapped in comfort, this cold embrace.
For in the winter's frosty hold,
Lies a beauty that never grows old.

Murmurs from the Frozen Tides

Waves crash softly on icy shores,
Murmurs linger behind closed doors.
Each tide carries a chilling rhyme,
Whispers of love, frozen in time.

The sea's deep breath, a breath of frost,
In its embrace, we count the cost.
Echoes of dreams in the ocean's song,
Drifting along where we belong.

Footprints etched in glistening white,
Marking paths lost to the night.
As shimmering stars reflect their glow,
Murmurs tell tales of hearts we know.

Beneath the surface, the secrets lie,
Dancing shadows beneath the sky.
The sea holds stories, both old and new,
In the frozen tides, our hopes renew.

Let the waves sing, let the night chime,
In this serene world, transcending time.
For in the quiet of winter's sway,
Murmurs guide us along the way.

Hushed Serenade of Winter

Softly the snow begins to fall,
Each flake a note in winter's call.
A hushed serenade, so tender and sweet,
Nature's rhythm, a gentle heartbeat.

Branches adorned with crystals bright,
Catch the gleaming of the soft moonlight.
In the silence, we find our place,
Wrapped in the warmth of winter's grace.

Frost upon windows, a delicate lace,
In every corner, winter's embrace.
With every breath, a chill in the air,
Yet love's warmth finds us everywhere.

Songs of the night on the whispers breeze,
Echo through pines, caressed by trees.
In these moments, we find our peace,
In winter's serenade, all worries cease.

Let the night be a canvas so grand,
Painted with dreams from a loving hand.
For in the hush, our spirits soar,
In winter's embrace, we long for more.

Crystalline Confessions

Beneath the frost, the secrets sleep,
Crystalline confessions buried deep.
Each shard of ice a whispered truth,
Tangled in memories of lost youth.

Sunlight dances on frosted ground,
Turning silence into sweet sound.
Reflections shimmer in the stillness bright,
Revealing wonders hidden from sight.

Snowflakes twirl like shy ballet,
Each a letter from skies of gray.
In their journey, they softly weave,
Confessions of all we dare believe.

Winter's breath wraps the world in calm,
A soothing touch, a gentle balm.
In the quiet moments, hearts will find,
Crystalline secrets intertwine.

So let us listen to the winter's song,
In nature's heart, we all belong.
For in the chill, connections grow,
In crystalline confessions, love will flow.

Snowflakes' Soft Confession

They dance from the sky, so light and free,
Falling softly, a wintry decree.
Each flake unique, a whisper of grace,
Telling secrets in delicate lace.

In the hush of the night, they subtly speak,
Of dreams and wishes, of hearts so meek.
With every flurry, they weave their tale,
In a shimmering coat, they flutter and sail.

The ground wears a blanket, pure and bright,
Transforming the world in silvery light.
As night drapes its cloak, the magic flows,
In Snowflakes' soft dance, love gently grows.

Listen closely, to the stories they share,
Each gentle fall, a heartfelt prayer.
Nature's soft sigh, a moment to cherish,
In their brief descent, all worries perish.

So let them land, let them twirl and spin,
For in winter's embrace, new journeys begin.
With Snowflakes' soft confession, we find our way,
In their tender whispers, we long to stay.

Whispered Dreams in Crystal Silence

In the stillness of night, dreams softly bloom,
Wrapped in silence, a fragrant room.
Each thought a crystal, refracting the light,
Whispered dreams take wing, taking flight.

Stars blink above in the vast open sky,
Cradling wishes, like lullabies nigh.
In the quiet, hearts learn to sing,
In the whispers of dreams, hope takes wing.

From shadows arise, visions so clear,
Guiding us gently, casting out fear.
In this moment, we close our eyes tight,
Wrapped in the warmth of the soft, starlit night.

Through the dark veil, directions emerge,
Muffled voices in unison surge.
In every small sigh, we discover our role,
Whispered dreams cradle the longing of the soul.

So listen intently, for magic's embrace,
In the silence, our memories trace.
With each fleeting thought, let spirits convene,
In whispered dreams, the world feels serene.

Frosted Whispers of the Night

Under the moon's gaze, whispers unfold,
Frosted sentiments, both tender and bold.
The chill in the air breathes life into frost,
In nature's own chorus, nothing is lost.

Trees wear a coat of glimmering white,
Embroidered with secrets of the deep night.
Each branch a canvas, a story untold,
Frosted whispers linger, gentle yet cold.

As shadows creep softly across the ground,
In hushed tones, the night is profoundly profound.
Breathless and eager, we wander and roam,
Finding solace in frost, far away from home.

Every glimmering flake has a tale to share,
With a touch of magic, they float in the air.
Together they weave a silvery thread,
In frosted whispers, the night gently spreads.

So let us embrace this serene, frozen view,
In the midnight stillness, we find something new.
With frosted whispers, the night sings its song,
In its cool embrace, we know we belong.

Veil of Silver Silence

A veil descends, wrapped in silver light,
Covering the world in tranquil delight.
Silence envelops each echoing sound,
In this quiet embrace, we are spellbound.

Muffled thoughts dance in the still, cool air,
A moment of pause, a tranquil affair.
Each breath a sigh, in the hushed twilight,
Veil of silence whispers through starry night.

Shadows entwine as the moon claims the throne,
Casting soft beams on paths unknown.
In the calm of the night, we find solace and peace,
As the weight of the day slowly begins to cease.

Each star a beacon, gleaming so bright,
Guiding lost dreamers through depths of the night.
In this sacred space, hearts find their tune,
Wrapped in the magic of a silvery moon.

So let us revel in this soft, sweet embrace,
With a veil of silver, we'll dance through this space.
In the stillness held dear, our spirits take flight,
Veil of silver silence, a world cloaked in light.

Frosted Echoes in Twilight

Whispers of night softly call,
Stars begin to rise and enthrall.
Frost paints the world in silver sheen,
Twilight dances, tranquil and serene.

Shadows stretch long on the ground,
In the stillness, secrets abound.
Echoes linger in the chilled air,
As twilight's magic we lay bare.

Moonlight glimmers on frosty leaves,
Nature's breath in the night weaves.
Each echo a story, softly spoken,
In twilight's embrace, hearts unbroken.

Time slows down, moments collide,
In the frost, magic and dreams reside.
A canvas of silver, whispers' flight,
Frosted echoes in gentle twilight.

As night deepens, we find our place,
In the quiet, we embrace grace.
Frosted echoes cradle our worries,
In twilight's arms, silence hurries.

The Air's Soft Conversation

Morning breaks with gentle light,
Birds chirp softly, taking flight.
The air holds tales of the day,
In whispers, it guides us on our way.

Leaves sway lightly in the breeze,
Nature's language puts minds at ease.
Each sigh of wind tells a story,
In the soft air, there's hidden glory.

Clouds drift lazily across the sky,
Watching as the world goes by.
The sun's warmth wraps us tight,
In the air's dance, everything feels right.

Hands outstretched, we catch the breeze,
Fleeting moments, like memories, tease.
Hearts whisper in the cool embrace,
The air's sweet conversation, our favorite place.

As shadows grow long, the day sighs,
In every gust, a secret lies.
The evening's hush brings calm reflection,
In the air's soft dance, we find connection.

Coated Dreams Under Glistening Skies

Beneath skies draped in shimmering light,
We wander lost in sheer delight.
Every step, a dream unfolds,
Coated in wonder, tales untold.

The stars twinkle like distant eyes,
Curating dreams as night supplies.
A blanket of warmth above us flows,
Coated in love, where the heart glows.

Gentle whispers drift through the night,
Encouraging souls to take flight.
Underneath this vast cosmic sea,
We dance with hopes, wild and free.

To glistening skies, we give our thoughts,
Wrapped in the magic that time forgot.
In dreams we wander, hand in hand,
Under celestial tides, we understand.

As dawn beckons with hues of gold,
We carry dreams, both brave and bold.
Coated in memories, we rise and sigh,
Under glistening skies, we learn to fly.

Traces of Frosted Echoes

In morning's light, shadows softens,
Frosted echoes, where time often coughs.
Each glimpse of light, a gentle trace,
Whispers of winter, a silent embrace.

Across the fields, glistening white,
Frozen tales in the first light.
Every breath a crystal sigh,
Chasing dreams where memories lie.

Footsteps print the frosty ground,
In stillness, a heartbeat sounds.
Echoes linger, a faint refrain,
Remnants of laughter in the cold rain.

The beauty fades as sun may rise,
Yet traces of frost still mesmerize.
In each fleeting moment, we reminisce,
Frosted echoes hold a gentle kiss.

As daylight grows, echoes may wane,
Yet in our hearts, forever remain.
With every dawn, there's magic anew,
Traces of frost shape our view.

Milton Keynes UK
Ingram Content Group UK Ltd.
UKHW010230111224
452348UK00011B/652